Skateboard Girl On the 5 Fulton, *Poems*

Lou Nell Gerard

Cyberwit.net
HIG 45 Kaushambi Kunj, Kalindipuram
Allahabad - 211011 (U.P.) India
http://www.cyberwit.net
Tel: +(91) 9415091004
E-mail: info@cyberwit.net

Printed at Repro India Limited.

Contents

Mom Had Alzheimer's, Revisited

If It Should Happen To Me

So baby if it should
Happen to me
Try these things

Bundle me up
Drive me round in the night air
In the Fiat
Top down
On Saturday and Sunday
Nights
"All Blues" blaring
On the radio

And if I can't ride my
Own motorcycle anymore
Strap me on the back
Of yours and go
Zoom
Carve some curves
Make sure I'm attached
And pop a wheelie for me

Lace up my Nikes
And lead me to run
Take me to music
And let me dance in the aisle

Drive me to magpies
With the air full of sage

And creosote bush
And let my hair blow

And please baby,
Don't dress me funny
Dress me in red and
Take me to bed and
Play that song and love me
"Like my backbone was yo' own"

And don't forget darlin'
Taj almost always makes
Me happy

There Every Day

Every day
Every meal

He was there
Sometimes just there and loving
Sometimes there, resigned and loving
Sometimes it was hard and the loving held him
Sometimes it just was and the loving held him

He was there to listen
Though her words were unintelligible sounds
He was there sometimes to talk to her
Though he knew not what she heard

He was there to sit holding her hand
In silence

He was there to follow her about the halls
As she sought the door knob that would turn
That would offer her door to freedom

Six years
He was there to simply be near her
He was there to pull out his pocket comb
And gently part and comb her hair
Every day

Gardening

Mom loved to garden, and more
She loved yard work, hard work
Sometimes to an extremely stubborn degree
Digging a tree stump up with a shovel
Over time, patience and stubbornness won out
A broken wrist in the mix

Then the Alzheimer's
And the sedentary silence

Six years
Each year I'd buy plants and seeds, my grand plans
Each year indecision caught me, mouth open
Pots and shovel in hand
Moving from place to place
No place seeming just right

Six years of plants dying in their pots
Seed packets gathering dust in lost piles
No collection of gardening books could help me to decide

Six years of not knowing if she knows me
Six years of expecting some shock to
Bring her back from her
What? Lonely journey?
Six years of mourning
Through six years of visits

Then pneumonia
Then she was truly gone
A brief sense of her return
Then recognition she was truly gone
We got her back
Briefly
Then lost her again
A memorial and gifts of potted plants

A rose a lovely orange to yellow sunset rose
And here, this is where it belongs!
Planted in the garden
Not withering in the pot

I bought plants and seeds
Into the ground they went
No hesitation
Everything had its place
Hello mom
Hello!

Transit Posts, Revisited

Skateboard Girl On the 5 Fulton

Skateboard Girl
On the 5 Fulton
Small, slim, long black hair
She boarded the 5 Fulton
Her skateboard almost as tall as she
Taller when she was seated
iPod
She was enjoying her music
The subtle movements
Trying not to dance in public
A favorite tune cracked a big smile
Head nodding
Any music lover recognizes the look of hearing a special song
She had brownies
Brownies in Tupperware
On the north side of Golden Gate Park
At the top of the hill
On the 5 Fulton
A native could tell me the bus stop number
Skateboard girl got off the line
Music, skateboard, and brownies in Tupperware
We got off partway down the hill
Walking back up
Backtracking
Here she comes!
Swiftly down the hill toward the ocean
Skateboard sound, hair flying
Music going, brownies in Tupperware
Smiling skateboard girl
Pure joy

The Gathering

The gathering
King County Pump Station
248 Park Lane
Students with Hello Kitty painted toes
Tech guy with his Razor scooter
Calloused chap with steel toed boots
It's the elderly couple's market day
Bottle caps and fast food wrappers building up
Like missed shots at the hoop of the garbage can
Crows have left the red onion behind
I wonder where the women are
Who sit like ancient birds of prey handing out pamphlets on the
northbound side
The 245 pulls up and we board
The blended scent of 18 different shampoos.
Strangers? Not quite

The girl with the bike at the bus stop with red lips

The girl with the bike at the bus stop with red lips
Looked up
Her shades had Balsa wood frames
Smiled at my purple boots
Went back one bus away
Racked her bike
On the 242
In her green helmet and
Pink ballet flats with a bow
and her red lips

Evening Commute

And everyone is talking on their cell phone
Loudly
Earnestly
Some are mumbling
And the baby makes a sound like a cat fight

She Dresses by Sun

She dresses by sun not temperature
What the hell
She's cute, probably knows it but not so's you'd know it
And face it
There are no goose bumps on that exposed spaghetti strapped
shoulder
Man with work boots and a backpack
Asks her "Aren't you cold?"
And it's not clear whether that was a fatherly question
Or harassment
But I detected no editorial nor lechery
She'll get off near the high school
He'll get off near the bowling alley

They both say thank you and wish a pleasant day to the driver

Winter In Summer

I sit on the sunny side of the bus
Pressed against the window as close as I can get
The sun helps alleviate the chill of the air conditioner
It is over 90 degrees out there
On the bus it is cold
The cougher sounds like winter

French Nails

She runs her French nails through her black hair
Past her silver earrings
Adjusts her hair clip
Does she think
She can get away with talking loudly on her cell phone
Because she's pretty?

Floppy Man

Loose and baggy
More backpack than he needed
It was floppy
He was floppy
His clothes hair pace hands
Hands flopped and he dropped
The sheet of paper he held loosely
His circular pacing made her nervous
Each loop came a little closer

John Hiatt through her earbuds
Reassured her
Her boots
She adopted a modified subtle warrior pose
Don't come any closer

Floppy loose looping pace
Closer
She side stepped further away
Into the open out from behind the bus
When he wasn't looking
I don't carry any money
Everything is on my phone
Including my music, you'll play hell
To get my tunes

In the backpack?
My lunch and the shoes I wear at work
Leopard print
Again you'll play hell to get those too

No no he is a restless
Harmless soul
He's not used to taking the bus
Maybe it's his first day at a new job
First in a long while
"Maybe it's his first time around"
Compassion
OK OK OK
Still caution caution
And distance

Here is the 245 bus driver
Loose man asks about the 238
Yes, yes, nervous
Restless nervous human
May your day go well

Improbable Shoes

Improbable Shoes
Incongruous with our clothes
Well-suited to walking
The occasional sprint
To catch the bus when the flashers go on
Our other shoes at work
In backpacks balanced on our laps
Tossed in a heap behind doors
Under desks
Stacked neatly on bookshelves
Tucked one atop the other in the back of a file cabinet
Or secure in a locker
All of us and our improbable shoes
Then...
She climbed aboard

6-inch stilettos
International Orange Baby!
Suede with a flash of orange
On the sole betwixt heel and toe
She sat and crossed her ankles
Our eyes fixed on those beautiful shoes
We missed her Mona Lisa smile

Slapstick

Running late for the 7:44 245
Pants on backwards
Too late to change
Juggling umbrella, gloves, earbuds, iPhone,
Backpack
An attempt to put the left-hand glove
On the right
Miraculously don't lose anything
On the fast tromp down the hill
Just miss the crossing light
Too many drive-to-kill commuters
To defy the red hand of "Don't Walk"
The voice from the pole commands "Wait!"
The 245 slips into Bay 4
The dash with the recalcitrant
Umbrella not ready to close
The mad dig for Orca pass
Tangles with the earbud wire
Popping the left one out
Climbing onto the bus
Listening to half music
Swipe!
No beep, no green light
Swipe! No beep no green light
The driver smiles
Points out the reader below
You've used countless times before
Swipe! Green light! Beep!
Smile back

Walk casually, sit daintily
In your favorite seat on the bus
And laugh at the slapstick of your own sweet life

English Haiku and Other Tiny Poems

Hatching

Baby spiders are
Hatching in veritable
Waterfalls, tumbling

Fretless

Fretless
A tuned ear
Ebony walk
Palpable sound
Boundless, boundless

Seasons

My feet were once tanned
Sunning out on our front porch
Now they're white and cold

Kiss

A puff of wind
Quaking Aspen leaves whisper
A kiss on my cheek

Faeries

Whirlwind, tiny leaves
Spinning whirling sparkling bright
They could be faeries

Two chairs

Face to face
Knee to knee
Dappled sun under ancient oak
Old friends

Oak Song

Ancient oak grand oak
Venerable oak shifts limbs
Woodwind notes oak song

Learning To Stop At Enough

Leaving, resisting
lonely in its lotus bowl
last edamame

When the Music Stops

Sometimes
When the music stops
I think I hear oboe
Low sultry intro notes
Slipping under the door
Like velvet
Like liquid
Like night

Hopeful Porches

New houses with hopeful porches
And front rooms eager for a view
Only to find a highway through the fog

Spotted Maple

Spotted Maple
Watches the birds and neighborhood cats
Waiting for an Amazon delivery
Tea roses
Their leaves, little hands touching the glass
Shield their eyes to reduce the glare
As they peer in the window

Vacant Boy

Those blue eyes
Disconnected
They belong to somebody's son
The eyes hint of a kind boy
But reflect a lost boy
A vacant boy

Girl On Hold

Girl on hold, girl on hold
Waiting until after
The promise of the one great "fix"
After which all will be well
She'll be unstoppable
Certain and sure
And decisive and motivated
After…

Evergreen Hula

Wind on the hilltop
Branches floating in the breeze
Hula dancers' hands

This, That, and the Other Thing

When the Wisteria Bloom

When the wisteria bloom
I know everything is going to be all right
We will see the rest of Spring
And Summer will follow

When the wisteria bloom
Bumble bees
The size of my thumb return
And delight the kittens in the window

When the wisteria bloom
And the bumble bees arrive
I know the hummingbirds
Are soon to follow

When the wisteria blooms
And the bumble bees delight
In its fragrance collecting pollen
I garden to the tune of their buzz

When the wisteria blooms
And the sun shines
And the Solari bells chime
I look at our Ashland hills

And smile

Crossing Normal

Crossing Normal
I smiled
The pre-dusk gold of the hills
The glow of the leaves
Like yellow sunshine
Like orange and red sunrise or set
No traffic coming down Normal
I pedaled across
Late late late October and it was still
Sunny and warm
Crossing Normal I felt the glow
Around me
I felt the glow inside
A realization
Here I was experiencing a part of my dream
Earlier this morning I wrote
And now I'm riding my bike
I didn't "should" myself out of either this time!
I came to Ashland for a multitude of reasons
Writing and riding my bike top o' the list
Crossing Normal I realized
It was OK to have done half the laundry
It was OK to have weeded half the raised bed
It was OK I was OK

Top of the 9th

Top of the 9th
Crows in the outfield
Sleek steel blue-black
Against glistening green
Seagulls in the infield
Whites grays soft seagull browns
Against wet red clay
Playing without stadium lights
Playing out of season
Strutting hopping pecking
The wind swallows the cheers
Of the ghost crowd
On the bleachers
One more out and the crows
Take home the trophy

Good Morning Sunshine

Where is my "Good morning sunshine!" friend?
This is how she greeted me every morning
I smiled
I felt like sunshine
No matter the weather
No matter the season
No matter my mood

I smiled in anticipation
Just to hear her say this
With her New England voice
With her own smile

"Good morning sunshine!"
She moved on
I moved on
Then one day a new person arrived
Fresh out of college
Bright
Smart
...and I found myself saying to her daily:
"Good morning sunshine!"
And her smile created it
Sunshine

I moved on
She moved on

Whatever happened to the summer of love?

Whatever Happened To the Summer of Love?
Peace? Compassion? Where?
Whence comes the divisiveness
Our bones are too tight, Wilma
Are we looking for someone to blame?
Creating our own fear?
Where does that kind of hate come from?
Not like me
"If you are not with us you are against us"
Bull!
It's the popularity of hate
Homogenize
Hypnotize
Kill debate
Still afraid of the monsters under our beds
We make them
Still afraid of the monsters under our beds
"We have met the enemy and he is us"
Still afraid of the monsters under our beds
We pull it out
"They, them, other are playing the 'N' card"
And thus we de-legitimize, devalue
So easy to say
We say it so ugly, so smugly
If it sounds cute, trite, sound bite
We pick it up spit it out
Spread it like wildfire
Spread it as truth
"Simplify and repeat"

"Popular talk show host said it?-—Check"
"Aligns with my prejudices?—Check—wait I don't have any
why some of my best friends are..."
"Fits my fear?—Check"
But remember:
"Fear always springs from ignorance." Ralph Waldo Emerson
And
"Fear is not in the habit of speaking truth." Publius Cornelius
Tacitus
Give me the girl in the old Don Henley song...
"Crazy people walkin' round with blood in their eyes
And all she wants to do is dance, dance, dance"
Maybe if more of us wanted to dance
We'd have less time to waste on hate

We Begin and We Are Invincible

We begin
And we are invincible

We proceed
And some of us are invincible
And some of us still do
Exercising cautions of experience
Anticipation of possibilities
And some of us grow leery

We persevere
And some of us tire

Further
And some of us get old before our time
And don't grow anymore
Crippled with fear
Caught in the tales of shoulds and shouldn'ts
Caught in the mire of feebleness that isn't real

We what?
Some of us remain
Who we are
Just a little older
Learning living doing
Maybe a little more cautious

Some of us what? Who? Why?
We don't become our mothers and fathers
Yet we joke that we do

Continue, continue, ahead
Stay out of the mire, the muck, stuck
Move, do, think, more than
Simply
Grow
Old

Guest Fly

We have this fly
A winter visitor
He's quite social
We seem to be his family
Bedtime we: people, cat and fly ascend
Up the stairs
He comes
Flying up up as we step up up
Never invading our personal space
As some flies do you know
Polite, he does not buzz us while we read in bed
He doesn't play his fly music inside the lampshade
Using his body to add rhythm to the echo
Of buzz buzz buzz
He prefers to fly quietly
In his own airspace
Until he sleeps on the ceiling
He joins us for breakfast
Blueberries his favorite
And after, when one of us gets up
He lights in the chair
Recently abandoned
Capturing the warmth
And sits as we read or write quietly
Lunchtime, into the kitchen
As sandwiches are prepared
Then low profile for the early afternoon
Do flies take siesta?
Later, again up the stairs

He joins us on the recumbent bike,
As we stretch on the foam roll
And he waits patiently whilst we shower
And flies his way downstairs as we head for our
Jigsaw puzzle,
Book,
Wine
Evening meal
Good night fly
One day we know his life span
Will have spun out
One night we'll head upstairs
We two people
Cat food and books in hand
Cat
No fly

Home, the Unexpected

Home
You know that place
Places really
Maybe you'd never been there before
Maybe you didn't want to go there
Be there
Maybe you were just ambivalent about going
Eh
Maybe you are only passing through on your way to someplace
ELSE!
Then there you are
You can breathe
That knot in your neck softens
You realize you are smiling and
Don't
Know
Why
Your posture is tall, strong
You are comfortable
You aren't worried about how to find that restaurant
Gas station
Grocery store
Beach
Coffee
It'll show up
You stop checking the time
Yelp
Facebook
Weather
Map

Mail
You're head is up
You are looking around
Taking it in
People say hello and you smile hello back
You are at ease
At ease
At ease
Home, you feel at home
Shh shh shh

It doesn't have to be a single place
Fixed in place
Fixed in time
It doesn't have to be where you were born
It doesn't have to be where you grew up
It doesn't have to be where you live now
Work now
That may not be home some of the time
On the interstate corridor
Surrounded by tired commuters
With their anger
Impatience
Frustration
Fear of driving
Stupidity
When you see the worst side to them
Your "neighbors"
But it may be even then
Even then
You look up
The eagle is sunning himself over the lake
The mountains gleam and shimmer white against blue
Sailboat sails are billowing

I Take Off My Glasses

I take off my glasses
And see dog faces
And benevolent monsters
Shadow boxing
In the fluffy evergreen tree boughs

Are they just as real as
Limbs and branches
And green needles
Blowing bouncing
In the wind?

They hear
My question
And answer
"Yesssss"

Night Terror

Should I have done something?
Something other
Other than lying in the dark
Sad and afraid
Fear and compassion joined
I sent him Maitri
"May he be free from suffering and the root of suffering...
May he know happiness and the root of happiness."
Neighbor boy grown?
New neighbor? No neighbor?
Visiting houseguest
For the long weekend?
Ex-soldier?
My immediate thought
PTSD
Military man
The voice:
Artificially stage-deep
Unnaturally deep and loud
Words paced almost evenly,
Not conversationally
Designed to be heard
Over the sounds of battle,
Gunfire,
Artillery blasts,
Loud chaos of battle.
Hard stiff words
Belted out in deliberate cadence
And style, yet,

I could not make them out...
Not trained to battle-speak?
Distance maybe? Context?
Anticipation: a single gunshot
The voice to cease,
Or gunshots and then what?
But sweetly, no.
Just silence.
I lay frozen not knowing
The right thing to do.
Is this how tragedy happens?
No one reaches out,
Makes a best guess and tries to help?
Then into silence a confusion
Loud TV or radio, then not.
Then the voice slightly subdued
Pitched as if in answer,
"You Do Not Understand.
You Do Not Understand.
You Do Not Understand."
Over and over and though quieter
I understood these words clearly.
More quiet still
Perhaps conversation though I never
Really heard another voice.
So someone was there or I invented someone
To let me off the hook for not
Helping a person in distress.
I could feel compassion—
While immobilized.
This didn't seem like a careless,
Stupid, drunk.
It was someone's son, brother, companion

Living a terror.
It was a call for humanity,
Empathy
In the dark.

Tunnel

Cars pulsing like bivalves under the tunnel lights.
They pulsed...like bivalves
In a mad scientist's laboratory
Just before they outgrew their aquariums
Glass bursting
Water seeping and splashing to the floor
The giant bivalves advance
Inexplicably no longer needing water
Through the lab room door
Leaving splinters
Ready to wreak bivalve havoc
Joining the cars in the tunnel
Pulsing and crushing and seeking
Revenge

Lost Uncle

I cannot hear his laugh anymore
I just realized in this moment
I cannot hear his laugh anymore
The memory always so strong
And comforting
My Uncle Buddy
I can still see him but
I cannot hear his laugh anymore

I feel lost
I cannot hear his laugh anymore
When did I lose it?
What happened to it?
Will I get it back?
What was the core that made it singularly his?

I strain to hear it but
I cannot hear his laugh anymore
Forty years gone I could still hear it
But now it is gone
How and why and I want that memory back

I cannot hear his laugh anymore
And that scares me a little
I cannot hear his laugh anymore
And that makes me feel the loss anew
I cannot hear his laugh anymore
And it feels a little piece is gone
A little peace

I flip through the visual images of him
The smells of him, his garage, his car
I cling to them
I grapple to recall it but
I cannot hear his laugh anymore

Is the time of mourning past?
At half-past forty years gone?
Then mom?
Then dad?

I cannot hear his laugh anymore

Mistaken Identity

Road work
Right lane closed
Cones
Heavy equipment, green
The city workers call it The Camel
The Camel was idling
Overlooking the hole
Where a lane used to be
A gathering
A discussion
A dispute?
If it were a real camel it would be grumbling
And settling in the sun to pose and chew
They are talking to someone
Someone down in the hole
He stands up
It's Tom Petty!

Pigeon Optimism

It was one of those "gift" days
It had been cold grey wet dark drear dank
Snow was in the forecast for the following day
But this day made yesterday seem distant past
And the next day was
Far off and improbable future
No one thought of yesterday and tomorrow on this day
It was clearly a day to experience as present as now
In the high 50s, downright balmy by comparison
The sun, unobstructed
The blue, a rich pure blue palette of blue on blue
Endless sky
Even the most perpetually disgruntled of people
Found themselves
Almost
Behaving well and feeling some strange
Unfamiliar emotions towards her fellow man
Yes I say!
Tenderness, kindness
The freeway pigeons were given to flights of fancy and fantasy
One flew from its perch under the overpass
And soared above and across four lanes
"Look at me! Look at me! I'm soaring like a crow, like a...
Oh! Oh! Ohoh!" Flapflapflapflapflap Flap!

Place Between the Ears

Place between the ears
If allowed there you are family
It is always the perfect temperature
Soft
It carries and shares
The scent of outdoors
Sun, rain, breeze, garden
All collected and merged
The best smelling fur
The soft
The warmth
The cool
And settled in that place
That home
Two ears caress
A purr gently seeps into the soul
Sweet center of calm

Spring in Seattle

Untamed body parts spilling out of young girls' short shorts
Grandmother in her long sleeve red sweatshirt
Woman striding, long beat gen hair pulled back
Jeans and jacket a walking cool beauty with her dark shades

Hounds everywhere mouths stuffed with tennis balls and tugging
on leashes

And the young couple triumphant in the city
In the filtered afternoon sun
Swinging their bag of Sunday fried chicken
From the Icon Grill

Guardian Dragon

It is the very core I need to look at
The Dragon's Eye
The Dragon's Open Eye
I must look at
And greet
And accept
And not fight
The Dragon's Eye of anxiety
Deeper than the pain
Deeper than the fear
Deeper than the lack of understanding
The Dragon's Eye
And this dragon
Is wearing full armor
No breaks
No holes
No chinks
No flaws
It is her very skin
And she is doing her job
She is protecting her treasure
And the treasure is me
She is my protector
She is my guardian
My alarm system
My survival mechanism
My anxiety
My fight, flight, freeze

I must not fear her
I must not fight her
Nor shun her
I welcome her
I welcome her
I welcome her

She may overreact
She may roar false alarms
She may perceive danger where there is none
Yet
She is doing her job
As my protector
My guardian
Her nature is good
And she always has the trump card
She will win the Scrabble game
I will love her
And befriend her
And accept her
But, hmmmm, but
When she overreacts
When the false alarms
Are roaring in flames from her
I will not fight nor struggle nor resist nor raise the ante
I will simply smile lovingly at her
And let go our embrace

What Happens

What happens when they get tall and gangly and awkward
And want piercings, plugs, tattoos or get teased because they don't
When they aren't cute, cuddly, malleable

Don't flip the switch on them
Don't turn out the lights

What happens when they eat everything
The cake you were planning to serve for dessert
The leftover chicken you were going to toss in the salad
And then they eat all their dinner and seconds and don't gain
weight
They just get taller and ganglier
Their faces break out

Don't punish them for their non-crime of hunger and growing
And trying to figure out all this in-between stuff
Yesterday you loved them
You saw them as cute
Now you can't pick them up
This is not their doing
Nor yours

What happens when they have opinions
And maybe they are not yours
When their hair gets long, or shaved off
Or turns teal, pink, orange

Love them still
Your child your child still and always

Work Stoppage

Blonde
Red
Brunette

Right through the middle
Of the construction zone

Girls
Young women really
Skinny jeans and spike heels
Delicate blouses
Carrying their individual pizzas
Back to their desks
Oblivious to the
Havoc they have wreaked
On the road crew

White Girl

Not that long ago
Not far far away
Here on the west coast
Forward, diverse, free-to-be-me west coast
Culturally open west coast
We sat in the restaurant
Over several tables
Our group from the conference
But I sat at the invisible table
We weren't getting served
We waited patiently
This is the laid back west after all
Finally because we did have a schedule
I beckoned a waitress
Who reluctantly came our way

I didn't understand her reluctance
Her acting like we weren't there
Even as she took our order

"It's me" Arden said
"Huh?" I, baffled
She pinched her black skin
"It happens all the time."

When the Nightmares Come

When the nightmares come
Do you let them pass?
Do you wake him?
Do you wake her?
Do you wait?
Do you wonder?

When the nightmare comes
And the cry is full of pain
And the cry is full of shock
And the cry is full of fear

Do you worry?
Do you debate?
Must it run its course?
Will he find resolution in the dark night?
Will she find resolution in the dark night?

When the nightmare comes
Do you wake him?
Do you wake her?
And then...
Will the ghost of the nightmare rejoice?
Will the ghost of the nightmare remain?
And subtly darken the day with a vague dread
A hesitation, just out of reach

So when the nightmare comes
You do not wake him

You do not wake her
And you hope he finds resolution
And you hope she finds resolution
And he wakes
And she wakes
To no ghosts, no dread, no vagaries

Or is it cruel?
Is he abandoned and alone in nightmare?
Is she abandoned and alone in nightmare?
Is there no resolution?
Only escape?
Will nightmare haunt the day anyway?

So you cling to the teddy bear
You cling to the hope
That you are doing the right thing

When Gray Turns To Gold

When gray turns to gold
Shu Lien's fur
When gray turns to gold
And golden brown
In the sunrise
The fur ripples
And shines
The cat squints
Into the sun
Feline smile
Whiskers blazing
With captured sunlight
Feline cheeks
Puffed with pleasure
Crow raven room
This morning I saw
Venus and Jupiter
In the pre-dawn sky

Waiting To Begin

And there she sits
Immobilized
Until
Until
Until
The sun comes out
The planets align
The eagle passes overhead
In a southerly direction
The planets align
The fever passes
The pain stops
The rain stops
The clouds break up
The sun comes out
Her lips are turning thin
She waits
And there she sits
Immobilized
Stagnant
Unrealized
Waiting to begin

Pandora

The packaging
Is coming loose
The cellophane is torn

Whatever control
I feel it is worn
Whatever it was that
Held me in check
Stayed me a good girl
I feel it slip

From time to time
The slut peeks through,
She almost drools
She lusts,
She's almost crude
She's sly
She writhes
Put her back in her box
I fear
She must be stopped

Unfinished Sentences

Tongue tied
Tongue tied
I speak in fits
And starts
Editing
Second guessing
Trying striving to say it like
I "should"
Random half sentences
Without end
I sound like an idiot
A prisoner of trying to please
Impress fit in win blend bend
Fuck it
Don't try to trip me up
It's already been done

The Girls

They walked off down the sidewalk,
Just like the girls they always were.
Chatting,
Wearing blue jeans, and favorite shoes.
Looking around, interested, listening,
One had taken off her jacket and tied the sleeves around her
waist
In a classic butt wrap style she'd affected since she was a little
girl.
It's only practical, right?
They walked side by side
Then one in front of the other
Sidling through other pedestrians where the sidewalks
Were crowded.
Pointing with their still hot lattes,
At the hills?
Laughing together at something.
New? Shared old memory?
Animated conversation, young eyes, young gait.
Gray hair, smile lines, cool looking shades.
Childhood friends?
It would seem so.
Hometown girls?
Sure.
Paused at the crosswalk until traffic stopped.
They crossed a street they've crossed before
Hundreds of thousands of times.
Maybe even in a stroller,
Maybe making wedding plans

Maybe pushing strollers side-by-side
Maybe...
They reached the other side of the street,
One passed her latte to the other
Took off her jacket, butt wrapped it
Recovered her latte and
They walked off down the sidewalk
Just like the girls they always were.

Roadtrip, Through the Windshield

The dirty fog went on mile after mile
Hung there so long you kept cleaning your glasses
Thinking they were smudged
After about a dozen cleanings
Upon closest scrutiny
You accepted that they were clean
Began to feel like your vision was getting worse
While you watched and waited for the fog to burn off

Dark gray Westfalia
With a crazy load of bicycles
Strapped on at cattywhompus angles
And an "Official Schwinn Dealer" sticker
On the side window
Driven by a likable looking person,
But also incongruous somehow
With her delicate fingers
Finished by pointy pink and green nails
Leaning forward
In Ichabod Crane posture
Looking a little nervous,
Bleached blonde hair
Fading to pink
Then green
Ending just below her ears
Cute but the thought
"Looks like a truck stop hooker"
Crossed my mind, not at all derogatory
But then I realized I had no idea

What a truck stop hooker looks like.
Probably just like any of us bipeds
Trying to make a living.

The double tag dirt hauler had bells on it.
We leapfrogged in adjacent lanes.
If you closed your eyes
You could almost imagine being on a pastoral hill
With sheep grazing in the sun
Rather than rolling down the I-5 corridor.
Well, except for the tire treads on highway
Windshield wipers and engine noise...

Off center pigtail like on a Yorkshire terrier changes lanes

She was such a bad driver that she held the steering wheel in one
hand and clutched the "oh my golly" strap in the other.

Cab of pickup truck packed to the brim with cowboy hats

The person in the car behind me had a face crafted by Munch.

The car was blue.
Everywhere.
Not automotive paint blue.
It looked exactly like
A blue I used when I was a kid
Making Christmas ornaments.
I remember the sound of the beads
In the spray can when I shook it.
Wheels too, blue
Some sort of faux moose catcher thing
Mounted on the front in place of a bumper.

Blue.
Mid 70s. Mid size
Sort of wallowing along.

The gray was broken by a brief thin spot in the clouds then a bit
of sun. Just enough to light up the hill of blooming Scotch Broom
just south of the Nisqually. Then rain came.

The woman in the car behind me
Had a gigantic apple fritter.
She was holding it up in front of her
Like an icon in the sun.

Taillights that look like Snidely whiplash's mustache
Other car light designs that look
Like they were done using the iron filings & magnet toy, Wooly
Willy

For sale. Gas hog w/ashamed to be seen in public windows

A blond smoker driving like a bat outta hell in a white Subaru.

Device

Whatever happened to "be here now"?
Just be
Just be here
In the moment
Smell the scents
Feel the breeze
See the nuanced shapes in clouds
Or in shadows
Varied blues
In different portions of the sky
Fancy flying crows
Sidewalk pigments
Out of state plates
People and things
Eye contact?
Too scary?
Device is not your friend
Not life nor breath
No opinions does it share
No true solace does it give
It will tell you your bus is late
It will give you music
And a book
And a movie review
It will buy you a ticket
And a latte
It will give you hope of fine weather tomorrow
It will give you a semblance of contact
With friends afar
Just a thing

A useful thing
Nice to have
Beware the hiding place
Beware its "concrete and barbed wire"
It won't enjoy a particularly lovely sunset
Or share the smile on a girl's face
The way her hair blows and the sun catches a glow
Or the way the man pats his dog, gives him a treat
Talking softly to him
Or the cat peering at you from a sunny window box
Three stories up and then blinking
It won't keep the low branch from scratching your face
Or share its coat with you when you are cold
Tactile, sure
But it won't return the warmth or cold of another hand
Or squeeze back
It is it
Not I
Not me
Not we
Not thee
Not he she them they
It
Or on your own?
Hear your own breath
Alone is not desolation
Idleness not despair
A moment
A pause
Time to think your own thoughts
See hear feel touch smell be
Try a moment of
Being
Here
Now

oad osed head

The gaps in the concrete
Of the in-progress overpass were filled in
With old bits of sign.
Seen from the train underneath
You could read an upside down "Left Lane Closed Ahead"
And "No Left Turn"
And in smaller gaps
"No arki" and "oad osed head"

The Woman I Talk To

The woman I talk to
Once a week
Never let's me off the hook

The woman I talk to
Once a week
Has a sense of humor
She has to
Else it just wouldn't work

The woman I talk to
Once a week
Sees things in me
Things I reveal without
Awareness

The woman I talk to
Once a week
Is sharp and quick and bright

The woman I talk to
Once a week
Questions and digs
Excavates

The woman I talk to
Once a week
Suggests
With insight

The woman I talk to
Once a week
Pries parses pares
Simplifies then clarifies
Simple? Yes,
Easy? By no means

The woman I talk to
Once a week
Friend?
Certainly not foe

The woman I talk to
Once a week
Guide? Escort? Usher?
For me, to me?

The woman I talk to
Once a week
Is there every week
For me
Except when she
Is in Maui

Refuge Under My Bed

Where do they come from?
The monsters under the bed
The monsters in the closet
Whom do they choose?
How?
I don't remember having monsters
I don't think I did
I had books and stories
And sometimes I simply felt alone
And sometimes I would listen to the night
Perhaps my beagle kept the monsters at bay
Are they a construct of the adult mind
So expecting the child to have monsters
They generate them unwittingly
And visit them upon their children?
To one who didn't have monster
Visitations they seem almost
Cliché
Passé
But not to those who are afraid
My monsters were not under the bed
Lawn mower
Vacuum cleaner
Sirens sirens sirens
Sent me under the bed
Under the bed
Cover my ears tight, still
It hurts it hurts it hurts
The noise

The fear
Maybe there were monsters under my bed
Guardians, protectors with whom I'd take refuge
Refuge under my bed

Rainy Drive

The splash of skin
That has lost its pigment
On the back of his right wrist
The crescent moon scar
One inch forward
Back of his right hand

Leaning roadside crosses
Holding up flowerless
Brown stems and stalks
One has been flung
Into the woods
White paint smudged
By an errant blue car

The pearl white Quest
Driven by an Asian child
Steady in the next lane
More aware of
Traffic surroundings road
Than most of the other drivers
Who actually had a driver's license
He used his mirrors
Active eyes
Just a boy
And why is he driving
Alone in the rain
Alone in the rain
Alone in the rain

Poor November

Poor November
Pumpkins find themselves helpless
Tossed into the street
Smashed and run over by traffic
Or simply left unlit
By the door where
They begin to cave in on themselves
Mimicking faces of great grandparents
And old men and women without teeth
Poor November
Once sunshine-bright leaves
Fall to the ground
Blown, raked, vacuumed, mulched,
Or worse—left to lie
Sodden by rain
Decayed into slurry
Trees stand stark naked and gray
Poor November
Her days are shorter and shorter
She ushers in cold, gray, rain
Rain is too late too late
For the raging forest fires of summer
And ushers out
Baseball and motorcycle racing
Poor November
Few people love November
Many dread it
Dislike it
SAD spikes in her middle

Some of us regain our morning light
Only to give up our long afternoons
Darkness falls early and we panic
Poor November
We give thanks one day
Succumb to greed the next
Poor November